Hal Leonard Student Piano Library

Piano Solos

Book 2

Authors
**Barbara Kreader,
Fred Kern, Phillip Keveren**

Consultants
Mona Rejino, Tony Caramia,
Bruce Berr, Richard Rejino

*Director,
Educational Keyboard Publications*
Margaret Otwell

Editor
Anne Wester

Illustrator
Fred Bell

To access audio visit:
www.halleonard.com/mylibrary

Enter Code
3981-3557-5017-0535

FOREWORD

Piano Solos presents challenging original music that coordinates page-by-page with the **Piano Lessons** and **Piano Practice Games** books in the **Hal Leonard Student Piano Library**. The outstanding variety of composers and musical styles makes every solo an important piece in its own right – exciting to both performer and listener. In addition, each piece is designed to encourage and ensure further mastery of the concepts and skills in the **Piano Lessons** books.

May these **Piano Solos** become favorite pieces that delight all who hear and play them.

Best wishes,

Barbara Kreader   Fred Kern   Phillip Keveren

Book: ISBN 978-0-7935-6267-1
Book/Audio: ISBN 978-0-634-08981-7

HAL•LEONARD®
CORPORATION
7777 W. BLUEMOUND RD. P.O. BOX 13819 MILWAUKEE, WI 53213

Visit Hal Leonard Online at
www.halleonard.com

Piano Solos Book 2

CONTENTS

* Students can check pieces as they play them.

Magnet March

Stepping steady

Phillip Keveren

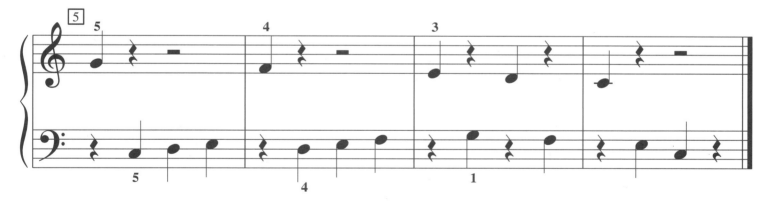

Accompaniment (Student plays one octave higher than written.)

Stepping steady (♩ = 120)

3

Song Of The Orca

slur = play legato connected

Singing, with mystery

Phillip Keveren

mf Come and play with me, Jes - sie, Jes - sie.

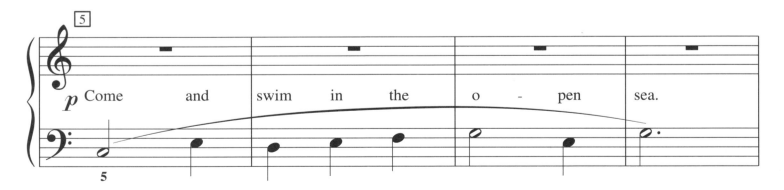

p Come and swim in the o - pen sea.

Accompaniment (Student plays two octaves higher than written.)

Singing, with mystery (♩=125)

mp   *p*

Ride with me to our se - cret is - land.

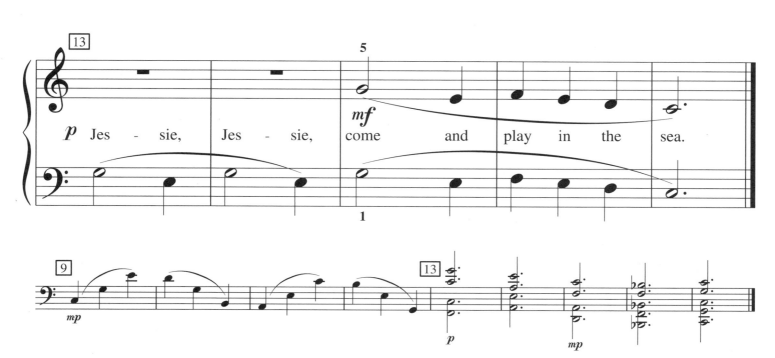

Jes - sie, Jes - sie, come and play in the sea.

The Macaroni Cha-Cha

With gusto   ♩=168

Phillip Keveren

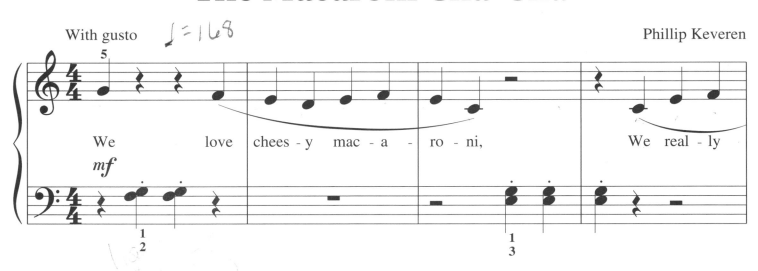

We love chees-y mac-a-ro-ni, We real-ly

LOVE that chees-y mac-a-ro-ni. (Cha-cha-cha.) Well,

Accompaniment (Student plays one octave higher than written.)

With gusto (♩ = 190)

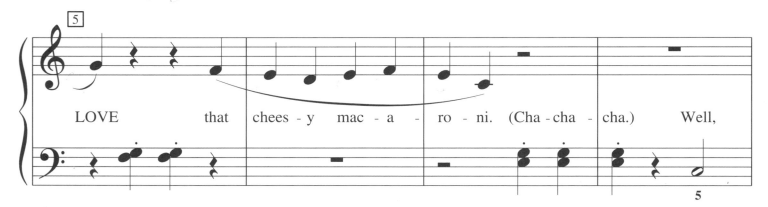

7

The Stream

Gently rippling

Phillip Keveren

Accompaniment

Gently rippling ($\quad$ = 130)

Play 8va throughout

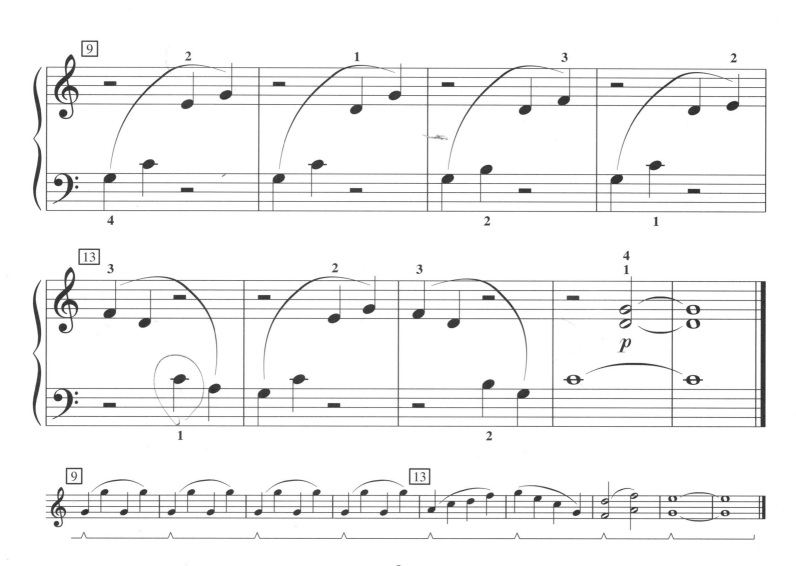

Leaps And Bounds

Moderato (♩ = 155)

Italo Taranta

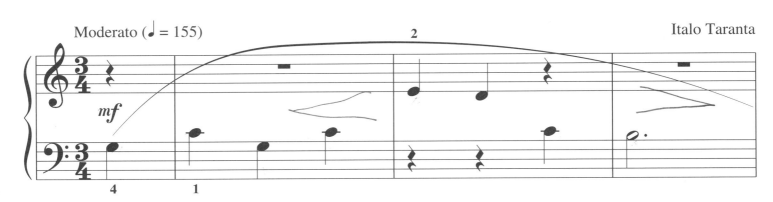

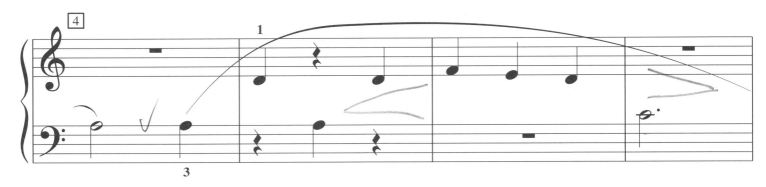

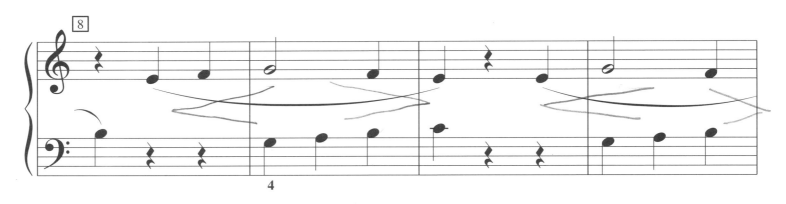

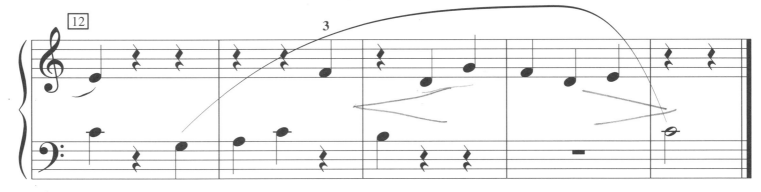

Tender Dialogue

Moderato

Italo Taranta

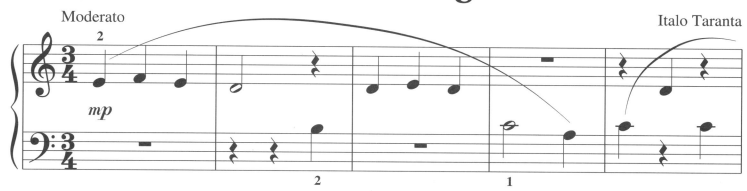

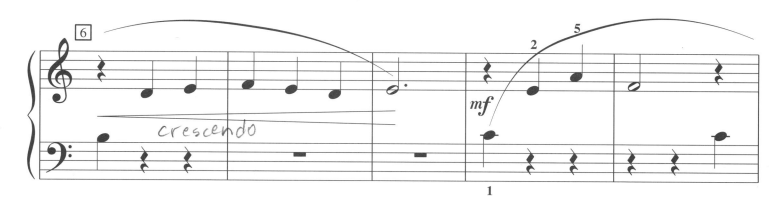

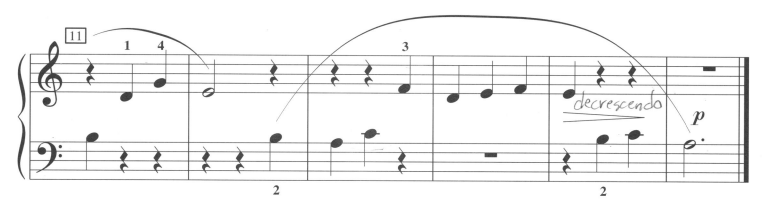

Accompaniment (Student plays one octave higher than written.)

Moderato (♩ = 112)

11

Use with Lesson Book 2, pg. 16

Dance Of The Court Jester

With humor 𝅝 = 140

Bill Boyd

Accompaniment

With humor (♩ = 160)

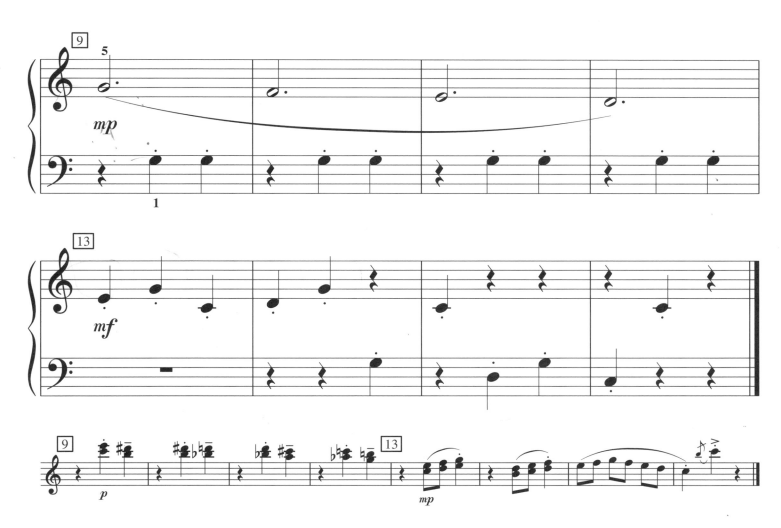

Tribal Celebration

Christos Tsitsaros

Accompaniment (Student plays one octave higher than written.)

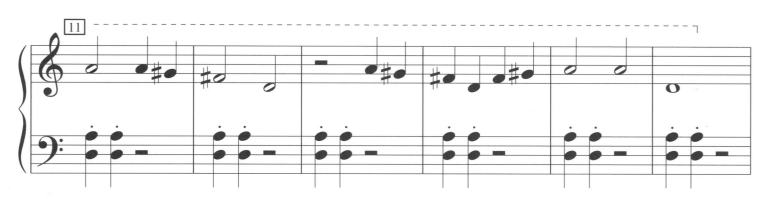

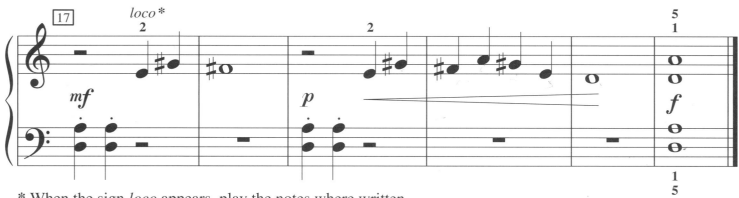

* When the sign *loco* appears, play the notes where written.

The Accompaniment

Student Accompaniment

With energy

Bill Boyd

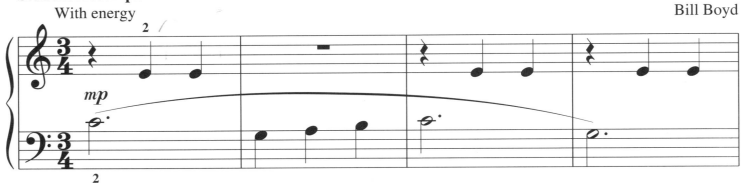

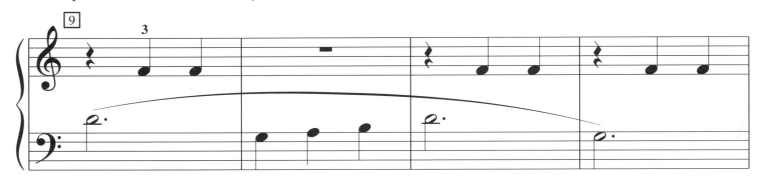

A sharp before a note lasts for only one measure.

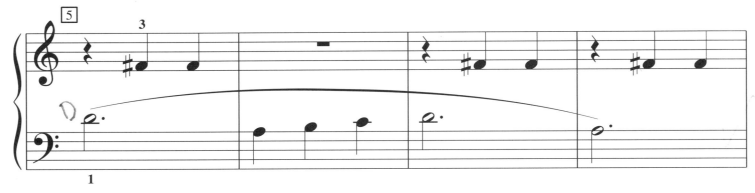

Teacher Solo (Student plays one octave lower than written. Teacher may play one octave higher than written.)

With energy (♩ = 175)

Take It Slow

Slowly (♩ = 85)

Bill Boyd

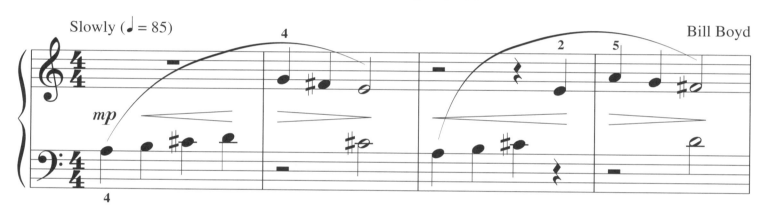

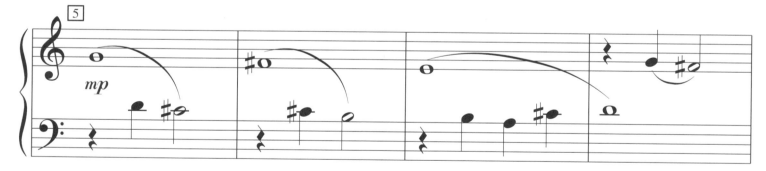

Accompaniment (Student plays one octave higher than written.)

Slowly (♩ = 85)

19

Viva La Rhumba!

Allegro

Carol Klose

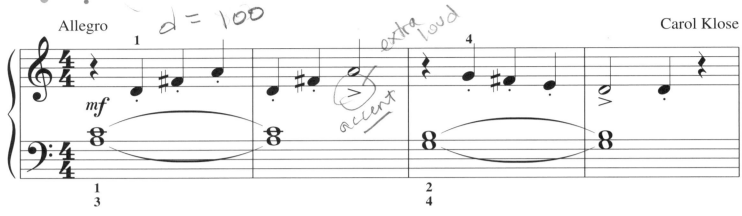

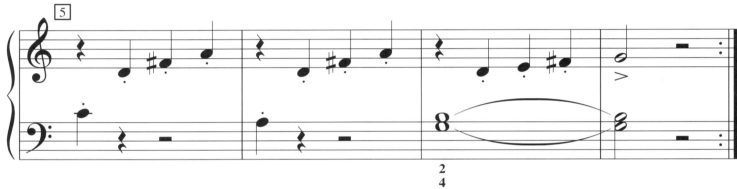

Accompaniment (Student plays one octave higher than written.)

Allegro (♩ = 120)

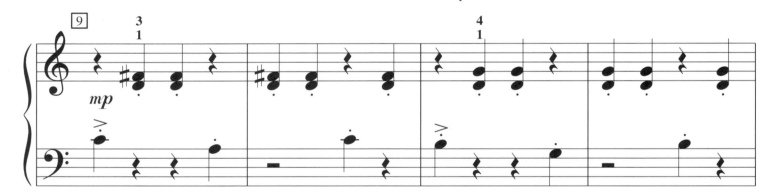

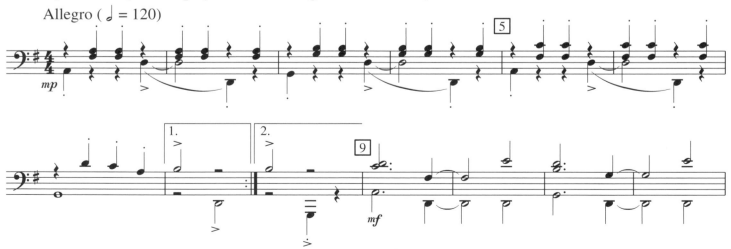

Grandmother's Lace

Flowing Waltz tempo

Carol Klose

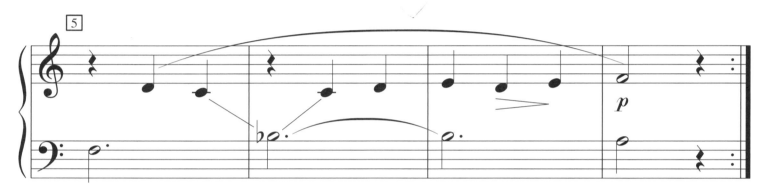

Accompaniment (Student plays one octave higher than written.)

Flowing Waltz tempo (♩ = 140)

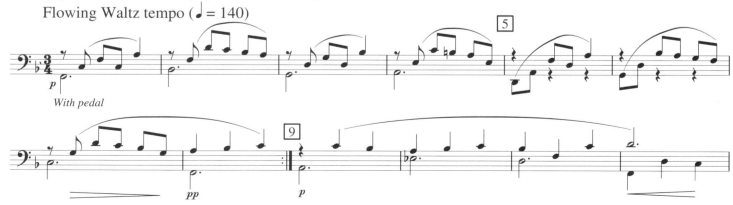

With pedal

Use with Lesson Book 2, pg. 34

22

gradually slower to the end

ritard

pianissimo

Those Creepy Crawly Things
On The Cellar Floor

Stepping very carefully (♩ = 140)

Carol Klose

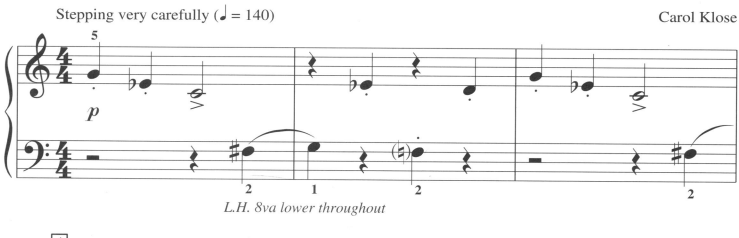

L.H. 8va lower throughout

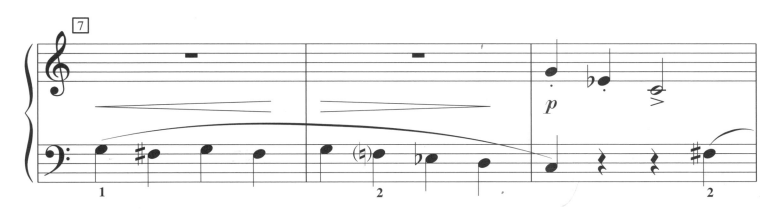

> Very high chord cluster,
> slap with R.H. palm.

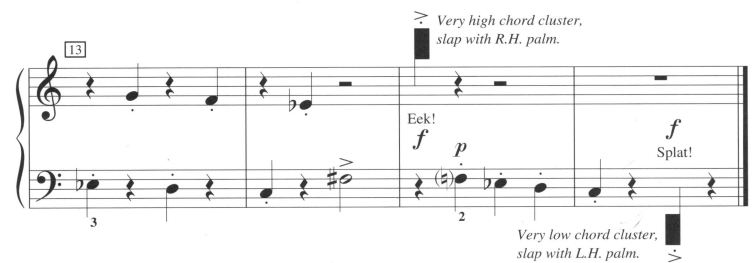

Eek!

f   *p*

f

Splat!

> Very low chord cluster,
> slap with L.H. palm.

On Fourth Avenue

Fred Kern

Leisurely, not fast (♩ = 120)

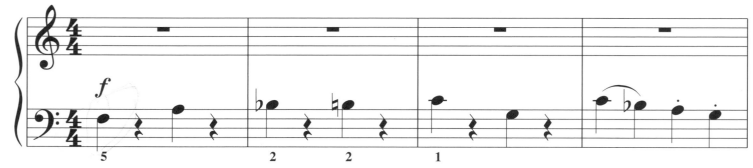

L.H. 8va lower throughout

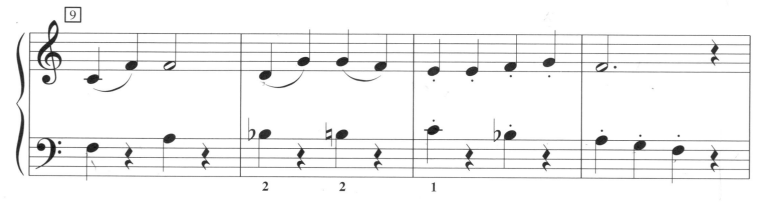

two octaves lower -

27

Goofy Gadget

Sputtering along steadily (♩ = 200)
Both hands 8va lower throughout

Phillip Keveren

School Is Out!

Fast Pop/Rock beat (♩ = 200)

Barbara Gallagher

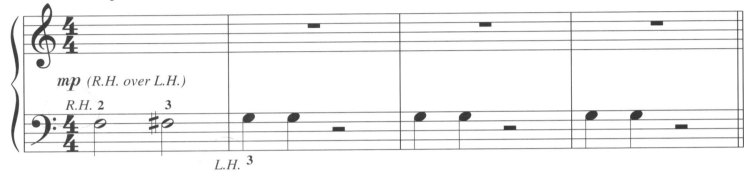

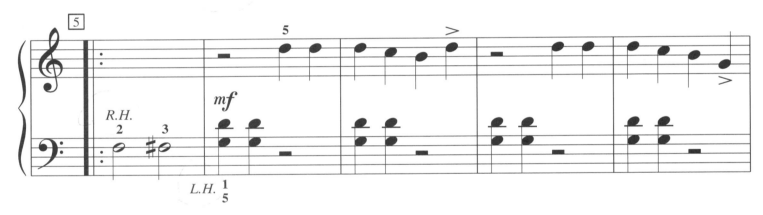

Hal Leonard Student Piano Library

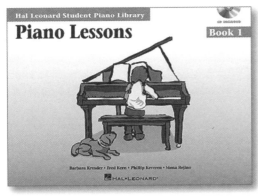

The Hal Leonard Student Piano Library has great music and solid pedagogy delivered in a truly creative and comprehensive method. It's that simple. A creative approach to learning using solid pedagogy and the best music produces skilled musicians! Great music means motivated students, inspired teachers and delighted parents. It's a method that encourages practice, progress, confidence, and best of all – success.

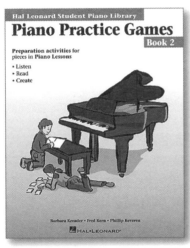

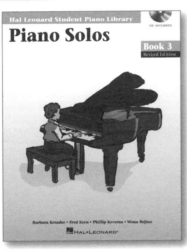

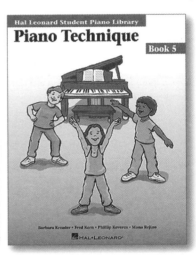

PIANO LESSONS BOOK 1
00296177 Book/Enhanced CD Pack $8.99
00296001 Book Only $6.99

PIANO PRACTICE GAMES BOOK 1
00296002 .... $6.99

PIANO SOLOS BOOK 1
00296568 Book/Enhanced CD Pack $8.99
00296003 Book Only $6.99

PIANO THEORY WORKBOOK BOOK 1
00296023 .... $6.99

PIANO TECHNIQUE BOOK 1
00296563 Book/Enhanced CD Pack $8.99
00296105 Book Only $6.99

NOTESPELLER FOR PIANO BOOK 1
00296088 .... $6.99

TEACHER'S GUIDE BOOK 1
00296048 .... $7.99

PIANO LESSONS BOOK 2
00296178 Book/Online Audio $8.99
00296006 Book Only $6.99

PIANO PRACTICE GAMES BOOK 2
00296007 .... $6.99

PIANO SOLOS BOOK 2
00296569 Book/Enhanced CD Pack $8.99
00296008 Book Only $6.99

PIANO THEORY WORKBOOK BOOK 2
00296024 .... $6.99

PIANO TECHNIQUE BOOK 2
00296564 Book/Enhanced CD Pack $8.99
00296106 Book Only $6.99

NOTESPELLER FOR PIANO BOOK 2
00296089 .... $6.99

TEACHER'S GUIDE BOOK 2
00296362 .... $6.95

PIANO LESSONS BOOK 3
00296179 Book/Online Audio $8.99
00296011 Book Only $6.99

PIANO PRACTICE GAMES BOOK 3
00296012 .... $6.99

PIANO SOLOS BOOK 3
00296570 Book/Enhanced CD Pack $8.99
00296013 Book Only $6.99

PIANO THEORY WORKBOOK BOOK 3
00296025 .... $6.99

PIANO TECHNIQUE BOOK 3
00296565 Book/Enhanced CD Pack $8.99
00296114 Book Only $6.99

NOTESPELLER FOR PIANO BOOK 3
00296167 .... $6.99

PIANO LESSONS BOOK 4
00296180 Book/Enhanced CD Pack $8.99
00296026 Book Only $6.99

PIANO PRACTICE GAMES BOOK 4
00296027 .... $6.99

PIANO SOLOS BOOK 4
00296571 Book/Enhanced CD Pack $8.99
00296028 Book Only $6.99

PIANO THEORY WORKBOOK BOOK 4
00296038 .... $6.99

PIANO TECHNIQUE BOOK 4
00296566 Book/Enhanced CD Pack $8.99
00296115 Book Only $6.99

PIANO LESSONS BOOK 5
00296181 Book/Enhanced CD Pack $8.99
00296041 Book Only $7.99

PIANO SOLOS BOOK 5
00296572 Book/Enhanced CD Pack $8.99
00296043 Book Only $6.99

PIANO THEORY WORKBOOK BOOK 5
00296042 .... $7.99

PIANO TECHNIQUE BOOK 5
00296567 Book/Enhanced CD Pack $8.99
00296116 Book Only $6.99

ALL-IN-ONE PIANO LESSONS
00296761 Book A – Book/Online Audio $10.99
00296776 Book B – Book/Enhanced CD Pack ... $10.99
00296851 Book C – Book/Enhanced CD Pack ... $10.99
00296852 Book D – Book/Enhanced CD Pack ... $10.99

HAL•LEONARD®
CORPORATION
7777 W. BLUEMOUND RD. P.O. BOX 13819 MILWAUKEE, WI 53213

www.halleonard.com

Prices, contents, and availability subject to change without notice.

0615